ZEN STICK

BY
RAHUL KARN

DEDICATED TO
ALL THE MEDITATORS OF PAST, PRESENT & FUTURE

PREFACE

Dear Zen Friends,

Thanks for welcoming the Zensational Stories series.
What comes to your mind when you hear the word "Zen"? Probably a peaceful monk or a meditating person at a beach!
You are right. But that is just one side of the coin. To attain to that peace, first one has to go through lot of adversities. To attain to awareness, one has to receive many whacks from a Zen Master whenever that student is dozing or slipping into thoughts.
In this volume, I have brought all those cases where a Zen Master uses his staff to discipline the student, sometimes the master even slaps the student! These materials have been compiled from different sources. Sometimes the same story is present in multiple ancient records. I have given a bibliography of resources at the end of the book.
If you are not familiar with Zen culture, these stories will look weird to you.
There is another specialty of this work. Unlike other volumes, I have not written any commentary on the stories, because the sound of raindrops does not need any commentary. Thus, this book is equally useful for new as well as old students of Zen!
Should you have any queries, please feel free to mail me on zensationalstories@gmail.com.
Have a Zensational time!

Yours Zen Friend
Rahul Karn
Melbourne
30th May 2019

Contents

PREFACE 5

1. The Taste of Banzo's Sword 11
2. Deshan's Blow 13
3. The Meaning 14
4. Trading Dialogue for Lodging 15
5. The Meaning 17
6. Hit 18
7. Any Difference? 19
8. Te-shan's Ultimate Teaching 20
9. Failure 21
10. Come Closer 22
11. Guizong's "One-Flavor Zen" 23
12. Knowing 24
13. Shit 25
14. The Whisk 26
15. Shilou's Shortcomings 27
16. Linji Holds Up His Fly Whisk 28
17. Ten Successors 29
18. Enlightened 30
19. No Worship 31
20. Dilemma 32
21. The Monk 33
22. The Meaning 34
23. The Short Staff 35
24. Shuzan's Staff 36
25. Hurt 37

26.	The Perfect Teaching	38
27.	The Jars	39
28.	What is it?	40
29.	Danxia Burns a Buddha Image	41
30.	The Great Meaning	42
31.	The Circle	43
32.	Can You Say It?	44
33.	Get Out!	45
34.	Changqing's Staff	46
35.	Heaven and Hell	47
36.	The Staff	48
37.	Blind, Deaf and Mute	49
38.	The Sutra	50
39.	The Word	51
40.	Ummon's Staff	52
41.	Thusness	53
42.	Calling	54
43.	The Buddhas	55
44.	Striking the Buddha	56
45.	Rinzai's Nap	57
46.	Source	58
47.	The Direct Approach	59
48.	Ciming's Bowl of Water	60
49.	The World-Honored-One's Lotus Eyes	61
50.	The Donkey Zen Master	62
51.	Hui-chung Expels His Disciple	63
52.	The Defilement	64
53.	Kao-ting Strikes a Monk	65

54.	Commitment	66
55.	Xinghua's Two Waves of the Hand	67
56.	Ho	68
57.	The Meaning	69
58.	Strike	70
59.	Please Express	71
60.	Inferior and Superior	72
61.	The Essence	73
62.	Huangbo Bows to A Buddha Image	74
63.	What is it?	75
64.	The Way of Going Beyond	76
65.	The Unapproachable Zen Master	77
66.	The Meaning	78
67.	Kill the Buddha	79
68.	Hsueh-feng Rejects a Monk	80
69.	Three	81
70.	Twenty Blows	82
71.	Guidance	83
72.	Knowledge	84
73.	Distinguish	85
74.	The Strange Book	86
75.	Beat Yourself with Stick	87
76.	Punishing the Sky	88
77.	I-chung Preaches Dharma	89
78.	Well-come or Ill-come?	90
79.	The Most Wonderful Thing	91
80.	Shoushan's Stick	92
81.	The Stick	93

82.	The Three Worlds Are Mind	94
83.	Staying in the Woods and Living on Herbs	95
84.	The Fist	96
85.	Guizong Holds Up a Fist	97
86.	Weight	98
87.	The Tao	99
88.	Fooling	100
89.	What is One Plus Two??	101
90.	You Idiots	102
91.	Fen-yang's Walking Stick	103
What Next?		104
Bibliography		105

1. The Taste of Banzo's Sword

Matajuro Yagyu was the son of a famous swordsman. His father, believing that his son's work was too mediocre to anticipate mastership, disowned him.

So Matajuro went to Mount Futara and there found the famous swordsman Banzo. But Banzo confirmed the father's judgment. "You wish to learn swordsmanship under my guidance?" asked Banzo. "You cannot fulfill the requirements."

"But if I work hard, how many years will it take me to become a master?" persisted the youth.

"The rest of your life," replied Banzo.

"I cannot wait that long," explained Matajuro. "I am willing to pass through any hardship if only you will teach me. If I become your devoted servant, how long might it be?"

"Oh, maybe ten years," Banzo relented.

"My father is getting old, and soon I must take care of him," continued Matajuro. "If I work far more intensively, how long would it take me?"

"Oh, maybe thirty years," said Banzo.

"Why is that?" asked Matajuro. "First you say ten and now thirty years. I will undergo any hardship to master this art in the shortest time!"

"Well," said Banzo, "in that case you will have to remain with me for seventy years. A man in such a hurry as you are to get results seldom learns quickly."

"Very well," declared the youth, understanding at last that he was being rebuked for impatience, "I agree."

Matajuro was told never to speak of fencing and never to touch a sword. He cooked for his master, washed the dishes, made his bed, cleaned the yard, cared for the garden, all without a word of swordsmanship.

Three years passed. Still Matajuro labored on. Thinking of his future, he was sad. He had not even begun to learn the art to which he had devoted his life.

But one day Banzo crept up behind him and gave him a terrific blow with a wooden sword.

The following day, when Matajuro was cooking rice, Banzo again sprang upon him unexpectedly.

After that, day and night, Matajuro had to defend himself from unexpected thrusts. Not a moment passed in any day that he did not have to think of the taste of Banzo's sword.

He learned so rapidly he brought smiles to the face of his master. Matajuro became the greatest swordsman in the land.

2. Deshan's Blow

Zen Master Deshan Xuanjian, whenever he saw a monk enter the gate, gave him a blow.

3. The Meaning

Someone asked, "What is the meaning of Bodhidharma's coming from the West?"
The Zen Patriarch Ma-Tsu hit him, and said, "If I don't hit you, people everywhere will laugh at me."

4. Trading Dialogue for Lodging

Provided he makes and wins an argument about Buddhism with those who live there, any wondering monk can remain in a Zen temple. If he is defeated, he has to move on.

In a temple in the northern part of Japan two brother monks were dwelling together. The elder one was learned, but the younger one was stupid and had but one eye.

A wandering monk came and asked for lodging, properly challenging them to a debate about the sublime teachings. The elder brother, tired that day from much studying, told the younger one to take his place. "Go and request the dialogue in silence," he cautioned.

So, the young monk and the stranger went to the shrine and sat down.

Shortly afterwards the traveler rose and went in to the elder brother and said: "Your young brother is a wonderful fellow. He defeated me."

"Relate the dialogue to me," said the elder one.

"Well," explained the traveler, "first I held up one finger, representing Buddha, the enlightened one. So, he held up two fingers, signifying Buddha and his teaching. I held up three fingers, representing Buddha, his teaching, and his followers, living the harmonious life. Then he shook his clenched fist in my face, indicating that all three come from one realization. Thus, he won and so I have no right to remain here." With this, the traveler left.

"Where is that fellow?" asked the younger one, running in to his elder brother.

"I understand you won the debate."

"Won nothing. I'm going to beat him up."

"Tell me the subject of the debate," asked the elder one.

"Why, the minute he saw me he held up one finger, insulting me by insinuating that I have only one eye. Since he was a stranger, I thought I would be polite to him, so I held up two fingers, congratulating him that he has two eyes. Then the impolite wretch held up three fingers, suggesting that between us we only have three eyes. So, I got mad and started to punch him, but he ran out and that ended it!"

5. The Meaning

A student asked, "What is the meaning of Bodhidharma's coming from the west?"
Zen Master Guannan Daochang held up his staff and said, "Do you understand?"
The monk said, "I don't understand."
Guannan hit him.

6. Hit

A monk asked T'ou Tzu, "All sounds are the sounds of Buddha-right or wrong? "
T'ou Tzu said, "Right."
The monk said, "Teacher, doesn't your asshole make farting sounds? "
T'ou Tzu then hit him.
Again, the monk asked, "Coarse words or subtle talk, all returns to the primary meaning-right or wrong? "
T'ou Tzu said, "Right."
The monk said, "Can I call you an ass, Teacher? "
T'ou Tzu then hit him

7. Any Difference?

One day Zen Master Deshan said to the community, "As soon as you ask, you've missed it. If you refrain from asking, you've also missed it."
Then a monk came forward and made a bow.
The master hit him.
The monk said, "I haven't even asked anything yet. Why did you hit me?"
The master said, "What difference would it make if I'd waited until you spoke?"

8. Te-shan's Ultimate Teaching

Hsueh-feng asked Te-shan, "Can I also share the ultimate teaching the old patriarchs attained?"
Te-shan hit him with a stick, saying, "What are you talking about?"
Hsueh-feng did not realize Te-shan's meaning, so the next day he repeated his question.
Te-shan answered, "Zen has no words, neither does it have anything to give."
Yen-tou heard about the dialogue and said, "Te-shan has an iron back-bone, but he spoils Zen with his soft words."

9. Failure

A monk came for instruction. Zen Master Nanyuan raised his whisk.
The monk said, "Today is a failure."
Nanyuan put down the whisk.
The monk said, "Still a failure."
Nanyuan hit him.

10.   Come Closer

A monk asked Zen Master Yunmen, "For whose benefit is it that you are teaching?"
The Master said, "Come closer and ask louder!"
The monk stepped forward and asked [once more].
The Master hit him.

11. Guizong's "One-Flavor Zen"

A monastic bid farewell to Zen Master Guizong Zhichang.
Guizong said to him, "Where are you going?"
The monastic said, "I am going to many places to study the five-flavor Zen."
Guizong said, "There is one-flavor Zen in my place."
The monastic said, "What is your one-flavor Zen?"
Guizong hit him.

12. Knowing

Zen Master Dogen once said:
I can remember, Yunmen asked Caoshan, "Why don't we know that there is a place of great intimacy?"
Caoshan said, "Just because it is greatly intimate, we do not know it is there."
Suppose this were Eihei (myself) and someone asked me, "Why don't we know that there is a place of great intimacy?" I would just hit his face with my whisk and ask him, "Is this knowing or not knowing?" If he tried to answer, I would hit him again with the whisk.

13. Shit

Master Xianqi of Heavan Child (Tiantong) Monastery (near modern Ningbo City, Zhejiang) was a disciple of Master Dongshan. Once a monk asked him, "I have come here for an understanding of the extraordinary teaching. Master, please give me precise instruction."
Master Tiantong said, "By shitting here, all is done. What kind of extraordinary and precise thing should I talk about?"
The monk said, "Since you've answered this way, I think I'll find some new sandals and go on traveling."
The master said, "Come closer."
The monk went closer.
The master said, "What's wrong with my answer?"
The monk didn't respond.
The master hit him.

14. The Whisk

Once a monk left Snow Peak and went to visit Master Lingyun Zhiqin, a disciple of Master Guishan, who taught in the same region of Fuzhou. The monk asked Master Lingyun, "Before the Awakened One was born, what was he?"
Lingyun lifted his whisk.
The monk asked, "What was he after he was born?"
Lingyun again lifted his whisk.
The monk then returned to Master Xuefeng on Snow Peak.
Master Xuefeng said, "You just left and you're already back. Isn't this too soon?"
The monk said, "Master Lingyun's answers didn't satisfy me."
When the master inquired, the monk told the story. Then Master Xuefeng said, "Put the question to me."
The monk asked, "Before the Awakened One was born, what was he?"
The master lifted his whisk.
The monk asked, "What was he after he was born?"
The master put down his whisk.
The monk bowed.
The master hit him.

15. Shilou's Shortcomings

Shilou was once asked by a monastic, "I don't know the original nature yet. Master, please show me by skillful means."
Shilou said, "I don't have earlobes [I have no ear to hear you]."
The monastic said, "I know I have shortcomings."
Shilou said, "This old monastic has faults too."
The monastic said, "What are your faults?"
Shilou said, "My fault lies in your shortcomings."
The monastic bowed.
Shilou hit him.

16.   Linji Holds Up His Fly Whisk

Linji saw a monastic coming and held up a whisk.
The monastic made a full bow.
Linji hit him.

17.   Ten Successors

Zen pupils take a vow that even if they are killed by their teacher, they intend to learn Zen. Usually they cut a finger and seal their resolution with blood. In time the vow has become a mere formality, and for this reason the pupil who died by the hand of Ekido was made to appear a martyr.

Ekido had become a severe teacher. His pupils feared him. One of them on duty, striking the gong to tell the time of day, missed his beats when his eye was attracted by a beautiful girl passing the temple gate.

At that moment Ekido, who was directly behind him, hit him with a stick and the shock happened to kill him.

The pupil's guardian, hearing of the accident, went directly to Ekido. Knowing that he was not to blame, he praised the master for his severe teaching. Ekido's attitude was just the same as if the pupil were still alive.

After this took place, he was able to produce under his guidance more than ten enlightened successors, a very unusual number.

18. Enlightened

Tianyi Yihuai (993-1064) traveled on to Cuifeng Temple in Suzhou, where he met the great Zen teacher, Xuedou Chongxian.
At their first encounter, Xuedou said, "What is your name?"
Tianyi said, "Yihuai."
Chongxian said, "Why isn't it Huaiyi?" [Reversing the order of the two characters of this name creates the Chinese word "doubt."]
Tianyi said, "The name was given to me."
Chongxian said, "Who gave you this name?"
Tianyi said, "I received it at my ordination nearly ten years ago."
Chongxian said, "How many pairs of sandals have you worn out since you set out traveling?"
Tianyi said, "The master shouldn't deceive people!"
Chongxian said, "I haven't said anything improper. What do you mean?"
Tianyi remained silent.
Chongxian then hit him and said, "Strip off the silence and there's a fraud! Get out!"

Later, when Tianyi was in Chongxian's room for an interview, Chongxian said, "Practicing like this you won't attain it. Not practicing like this you won't attain it. This way or not this way, neither way will attain it."

Tianyi began to speak but Chongxian drove him out of the room with blows. This unpleasant scene repeated itself four times. Some time later, while Tianyi fetched water from the well and carried it with a shoulder pole back to the temple, the pole suddenly broke. As the bucket crashed to the ground Tianyi was suddenly enlightened.

19. No Worship

Passing by the main hall, Joshu saw a monk worshipping. Joshu hit him once with his stick.

The monk said, "After all, worshipping is a good thing."

Joshu said, "A good thing isn't as good as nothing."

20. Dilemma

There was a master walking in the forest with a group of his disciples, and suddenly he picked up a tree branch and said to one of the monks, "What is it?" And the monk hesitated; didn't answer immediately, so the teacher hit him with it. So, he turned to another monk and said, "What is it?" And the monk said, "Give it to me, so that I can see." And the master tossed him the branch. He caught it and he hit the master with it. And so, the master said, "Well, you got out of that dilemma."

21. The Monk

Zen Master Xinghua Cunjiang (840-925 CE) asked a monk, "Where have you come from?"
"From master Cui's place," replied the monk.
"And brought master Cui's shout along too?" asked the master.
"That didn't come," replied the monk.
"If that is so, you didn't come from master Cui's place." said the master.
The monk gave a shout whereupon the master hit him.

22. The Meaning

A monk asked Zen Master Magu Baoche, 'Concerning the twelve-fold teachings, this fellow has no doubts, but what is the meaning of the Patriarch's coming from the West?'
The master stood up and with his stick drew a circle around him, lifted one leg in the air and said, 'Understood?'
The monk had no reply, so the master hit him.

23.   The Short Staff

Shuzan held out his short staff and said, "If you call this a short staff, you oppose its reality. If you do not call it a short staff, you ignore the fact. Now what do you wish to call this?"

24. Shuzan's Staff

Shuzan held up his staff and waved it before his monks.

"If you call this a staff," he said, "you deny its eternal life. If you do not call this a staff, you deny its present fact. Tell me just what do you propose to call it?"

25. Hurt

Once when Zen master Baofu Congzhan saw a monk he struck a nearby pillar with his staff. He then struck the monk on the head. The monk refrained from expressing pain.
Baofu said, "Why didn't that hurt?"

26. The Perfect Teaching

The master asked Pai-chang, one of his chief disciples: "How would you teach others?"

Pai-chang raised his hossu (A hossu is a short staff of wood or bamboo with bundled hair or hemp wielded by a Zen Buddhist priest. Often described as a "fly swatter" or "fly shooer", the stick is believed to protect the wielder from desire and also works as a way of ridding areas of flies without killing them).

The master remarked, "Is that all? No other way?"

Pai-chang threw the hossu down.

27. The Jars

Ma Tsu sent a messenger with a letter and a present of three jars of sauce to Pai Chang. After ordering the assistant to place the three jars in the Chan hall he ascended to his high seat, pointed his staff at the jars and said, 'If you can speak correctly, I shall not break the jars; if you do not speak correctly, I shall break them.'
The audience remained speechless and Pai Chang broke the jars of sauce and returned to the abbot's room.

[NOTE: The act of breaking the jars is the functioning of the mind and the act of returning to the abbot's room reveals the return of function to the substance of the mind.]

28. What is it?

Zen master Baizhang entered the hall to give a lecture. When the monks had assembled, he suddenly leaped off of the Dharma seat and drove them from the hall with his staff. Just as they were running out of the hall, he called to them. When they turned around, he said, "What is it?"

29. Danxia Burns a Buddha Image

Once when Zen master Danxia Tianran was staying at the temple Huilin si in the capital on a very cold day he took a wooden buddha image from the buddha hall, set it on fire, and warmed himself by the flames.

The temple supervisor happened to see this and scolded Danxia, saying, "How can you burn my wooden buddha!"

Danxia stirred the ashes with his staff and said, "I'm burning it to get the holy relics."

The supervisor replied, "How could there be relics in a wooden buddha?"

"If there are no relics," Danxia answered, "then please give me the two attendant images to burn."

30. The Great Meaning

Zen master Muzhou asked a monk, "Where do you come from?"
The monk said, "From Liuyang."
Muzhou said, "What does the teacher there say when a student asks him about the great meaning of the Buddhadharma?"
The monk said, "He says, 'Traveling everywhere without a path.'"
Muzhou said, "Does that teacher really say that or not?"
The monk said, "He really does say that."
Muzhou took his staff and struck the monk, saying, "This fool just repeats words!"

31. The Circle

One day a monk came to practice under Zen Master Yangshan. He asked, "Does the master recognize written characters?"
The master said, "I recognize some."
The monk then drew a circle in the air and presented it to Yangshan.
The master used his sleeve to erase the circle.
The monk drew another circle and presented it.
The master received it with both hands then threw it behind him.
The monk stared at the master. The master looked down.
The monk then walked in a circle around the master's seat.
The master then hit the monk with his staff.
The monk went out.

32.   Can You Say It?

One day when Master Guishan was walking on the mountain, he saw Huiji (Yangshan Huiji, who later on himself became great Zen Master) doing seated meditation under a tree. The master tapped Huiji on the back with his staff. Huiji turned his head, and Guishan asked, "Huiji, can you say it?"

Huiji replied, "Although I cannot say it, I will not depend upon someone else's mouth."

The master approved.

33.   Get Out!

Once a monk asked Zen Master Deshan Xuanjian, "What is awakening?"
Deshan struck him with his staff and said, "Get out, don't defecate here!"
Then the monk asked, "What is Buddha?"
The master said, "An old beggar in India."

34. Changqing's Staff

Zen master Changqing, taking up his staff, said to the assembly, "Know this, and you have completed a lifetime's practice."

35. Heaven and Hell

A monk asked Zen master Yangshan, "What is the difference between heaven and hell?"
The Master used his staff to draw a line upon the ground.

36.   The Staff

Zen master Bajiao held up his staff and said to the monks, "If you have a staff, I give you a staff. If you don't have a staff, then I take it away from you."
Then, using his staff for support, he got down and left the hall.

37. Blind, Deaf and Mute

Zen Master Xuansha gave instruction to the congregation, saying: "The great masters everywhere speak extensively of reaching and benefiting beings. If they encountered three persons with different disabilities, how would they reach them? For a blind person, if they wielded the staff or raised their whisk then the person would not see it. For a deaf person, if they spoke of samadhi, then he would not hear it. For a mute person, if they called on him to speak, he could not do so. So, what would they do to reach them? If these types cannot be reached, then the Buddhadharma has no effect."

38. The Sutra

Zen master Shishuang entered the hall and addressed the monks, saying, "All of the Buddhas, and all of the Buddhas' anuttara-samyakasambodhi (unparalleled perfect enlightenment), come forth from this sutra." He then raised his staff upright and said, "This is the Nanyuan Temple staff. Where is the sutra?"

After a long pause, he said, "The text is long. I'll give it to you later." Then with a shout he got down from the seat.

39.   The Word

Zen Master Shishuang entered the hall and said, "I have a word that cuts off thinking and leaves cause and effect behind. But even clever people can't speak it! It may only be transmitted by way of mind. There is another word that may only be directly expressed. What is the word that can only be directly expressed?"

After a pause, Shishuang drew a circle in the air with his staff. Then he shouted.

40. Ummon's Staff

Asked by a monk, "What is the doctrine that transcends all Buddhas and Masters?"
Ummon immediately held aloft his staff, and said to the assembled monks, "I call this a staff; what do you call it?"
The monk was silent. Again, Ummon held up the staff, saying "The doctrine transcending all the Buddhas and masters, -was not that what you asked me about?"

41. Thusness

When Mayu Baoche came to practice with the National Teacher, he circled the meditation platform three times, then struck his staff on the ground and stood there upright.
The National Teacher said, "You are thus. I also am thus."
Mayu struck his staff on the ground again.
The National Teacher said, "Get out of here, you wild fox spirit!"

42. Calling

Once Zen Master Yunmen said, "I used to say that all sounds are the Buddha's voice, all shapes are the Buddha's form, and that the whole world is the Dharma body. Thus, I quite pointlessly produced views that fit into the category of 'Buddhist teaching.' Right now, when I see a staff, I just call it 'staff,' and when I see a house, I just call it 'house.'"

43. The Buddhas

When Zen Master Shishi Shandao (781-872) saw a new monk coming by, he was often known to hold up his staff and say, "Awakened ones of the past are just this; awakened ones of the present are just this; awakened ones of the future are just this."

44. Striking the Buddha

When Zen Master Taego (1301-1382) was appointed as the abbot of Bongeun Seon monastery, he occupied the room of the abbot, picked up his staff and put it down once, saying, "If a Buddha comes here, I will strike him, and if a patriarch comes I will strike him."

He pointed at the Dharma-throne and said, "The innumerable Buddhas and patriarchs have shat here, filing the heavens with a stink and filing up the entire sahā (endurance of suffering) world. Today I cannot avoid pouring the waters of the four great oceans (over it) to wash and make it neat and clean. Great assembly, do not say it is even messier."

45. Rinzai's Nap

One day, Rinzai was taking a nap in the hall. When the master saw him, he tapped the couch with his staff. Rinzai lifted his head and, seeing that it was none other than the Abbot, went to sleep again. The Abbot, after giving another tap on the couch, went on. Finding the leader of his community sitting in meditation, he said to him, "The young fellow down there is seated in meditation, how is it that you are indulging in wild fancies here?"
The leader said, "Oh, this old fellow, what is he doing?"
The Abbot, tapping the seat once, went out. But what a strange lesson he had given! Sleeping is sitting in meditation, and sitting in meditation is indulging in wild fancies!

46. Source

When the Master Yangshan Huiji was carrying a staff in his hand a monk came to him and asked, "Where did you get this?" The Master turned it over and held it at his back. The monk said nothing.

47. The Direct Approach

A monk asked, "What is that direct approach to the Source to which Buddha would give his seal of approval?" At this, the Master Hsiang-yen Chih-hsien threw away his staff and walked out with his hands empty.

48. Ciming's Bowl of Water

One day in his quarters Ciming Chuyuan put down a bowl of water, placed a sword on top and a pair of straw sandals underneath, and sat down beside it holding his staff. Seeing a monk enter the gate, he pointed. When the monk hesitated, the master struck him.

49. The World-Honored-One's Lotus Eyes

Fengxue Yanzhao went to the hall and said, "The World-Honored-One looked upon the assembly with his blue-lotus eyes."
Then he asked, "At that moment, what was the Buddha teaching? If you say he was teaching by not teaching, you are slighting the Old Sage. So, tell me, what was he teaching?"
At this, Shoushan Shengnian shook his sleeves and left.
Fengxue threw down his staff and returned to his quarters. His attendant, following after him, asked, "Why didn't Shengnian answer you?"
"Because Shengnian understood," replied Fengxue.

50. The Donkey Zen Master

The Venerable Ximu of Yizhou (Sichuan, Chengdu) ascended the podium and a layman raised his hand, saying, "The venerable sir is just a donkey."
"The old monk is being ridden by you," replied the master.
The man had no reply and left. Three days later he came again and said, "Three days ago I came across a thief."
The master took his staff and drove him out.

51. Hui-chung Expels His Disciple

Tan-hsia paid a visit to Hui-chung, who was taking a nap at the time. "Is your teacher in?" asked Tan-hsia of an attending disciple. "Yes, he is, but he does not want to see anyone," said the monk. "You are expressing the situation profoundly," Tan-hsia said. "Don't mention it. Even if Buddha comes, my teacher does not want to see him." "You are certainly a good disciple. Your teacher ought to be proud of you," and with these words of praise, Tan-hsia left the temple. When Hui-chung awoke, Tan-yuan, the attending monk, repeated the dialogue. The teacher beat the monk with a stick and drove him from the temple.

52. The Defilement

Dahui Zonggao asked a monk, "The Way does not require practice, but it must not be defiled. What is the undefiled way?"
The monk said, "I don't dare answer."
Dahui said, "Why not?"
The monk said, "I'm afraid of defilement."
Dahui said, "Good! Bring in the broom for sweeping shit!"
The monk was flustered.
Dahui drove him out of the room with blows.

53. Kao-ting Strikes a Monk

A monk came from Chia-shan and bowed to Kao-ting.
Kao-ting immediately struck the monk.
The monk said, "I came especially to you and paid homage with a bow. Why do you strike me?"
Kao-ting struck the monk again and drove him from the monastery.
The monk returned to Chia-shan, his teacher, and related the incident.
"Do you understand or not?" asked Chia-shan.
"No, I do not understand it, "answered the monk.
"Fortunately, you do not understand," Chia-shan continued.
"If you did, I would be dumbfounded."

54. Commitment

In olden days Abbot Jimyo, sitting in meditation day and night through the bitter winter, found himself often invaded by the demon of sleep. He took a gimlet and drove it into his thigh with the words: "The light of the ancient sages was made great through piercing sufferings. Alive to achieve nothing, and to die unknown to any, what use is such a life?"

55. Xinghua's Two Waves of the Hand

A fellow student of Xinghua Cunjiang came and entered the Dharma Hall. Xinghua gave a shout. The monk too gave a shout and advanced two or three strides, whereupon Xinghua shouted again. The monk too shouted again, and after a moment came forward. Xinghua held up his staff. The monk again shouted.

"You see! This dolt is still trying to play the host!" remarked Xinghua. The monk hesitated. Xinghua struck him and drove him out of the Dharma Hall, then returned to his quarters.

Someone asked, "The monk who was just here—what did he say to deserve the master's anger?"

Xinghua answered, "That monk had technique, he had essence, he had illumination, he had function. But when I waved my hand in front of him two times he couldn't respond. If you don't hit a blind oaf like that he'll never get anywhere."

56. Ho

The Master Yangshan Huiji saw a monk coming toward him and lifted his fu-tzu.
[The fu-tzu (Japanese hossu) was the pointer used by the ancient masters as they gave sermons or led discussions. It was a short staff of wood, bamboo, or jade, with a brush of long hair at one end. It was first called chu-kwei after the large deer from whose tail came the hair for the brush; fu-tzu refers to the horsehair from which the brush was later made.]
The monk said, "Ho!"
The Master said, "To utter a 'Ho' is not nothingness. Tell me where is my mistake."
The monk said, "You, Master, should not depend upon objective means to reveal the truth to the people."
The Master immediately struck him.

57. The Meaning

The Master Hsiang-yen Chih-hsien asked a monk where he came from. He replied that he came from Kuei-shan. The Master asked what statement Kueishan had made recently. The monk replied that another monk had asked him about the meaning of the Patriarch coming from the West and Master Kuei-shan had held up his fu-tzu in response. When Master Hsiang-yen heard this, he asked what Kuei-shan's disciples understood by this gesture. His brother monks agreed, said the monk, that it meant that mind is illumined through matter and reality is revealed through things. The Master said, "Their understanding is all right as far as it goes. But what is the good of being so eager to theorize?" The monk asked him how he would have explained the gesture. The Master held up his fu-tzu.

58. Strike

Striking was used for many purposes. Sometimes it was punitive and sometimes not. For the uninitiated, the two are indistinguishable, but the enlightened know the difference. Once Hsueh-feng held up his fu-tzu and said, "This is for those who are inferior." A monk asked, "What would you do for those who are superior?" The Master lifted his fu-tzu. The monk objected, "But that is for those who are inferior!" and the Master struck him. Hsueh-feng's action seems to be identical each time he lifts the fu-tzu, but in fact it is quite different. The first time he raised it, it was to threaten those who did not have understanding and deserved a blow as punishment. The second time, it was symbolic of the great action, spontaneous and free, meaningless, and intention less, having neither subject nor object. This great action, derived from the center of Hsueh-feng's innermost being, serves as the answer usually given by Chan masters.

59. Please Express

A monk pleaded, "Master! Please express what I cannot express myself."

The Master Hsueh-feng I'tsun (822-908) answered, "For the Dharma's sake I have to save you!"

Thereupon he lifted his fu-tzu and flourished it before the monk. The monk departed immediately.

60. Inferior and Superior

The Master Hsueh-feng I'tsun (822-908) came to the assembly, lifted his fu-tzu, and said, "This is for those who are inferior." A monk asked, "What would you do for those who are superior?" The Master lifted his fu-tzu. The monk retorted, "That was for those who are inferior." The Master struck him.

61. The Essence

The monk Ting came to the Master Lin-chi and asked, "What is the essence of Buddhism?" The Master came down from his straw chair, slapped his face, and pushed him away. Ting, the questioner, stood there unmoved. A monk standing by said to him, "Ting! Why don't you bow to the Master?" As the monk, Ting started to make a bow he suddenly attained enlightenment.

62. Huangbo Bows to A Buddha Image

One day, when Zen Master Huangbo was bowing before a Buddha image in the Buddha Hall, the novice Xuan asked, "If we should 'seek nothing from the Buddha, seek nothing from the Dharma, and seek nothing from the Sangha,' then what does your venerable seek by bowing to the Buddha?"

Master Huangbo replied, "Seeking nothing from the Buddha, seeking nothing from the Dharma, seeking nothing from the Sangha - that's how I always do prostrations."

"Why bow then?" Xuan insisted.

Master Huangbo slapped the novice.

"How rude!" Xuan said.

"What sort of place is this to be talking about rudeness or courtesy?" Master replied and he slapped Xuan again.

63. What is it?

A monk knocked on Zen Master Muzhou's door. The Master asked, "What is it?"
The monk answered, "I do not yet understand my own affairs of life and death. Please, Master, guide me."
The Master replied, "What I have for you here is a stick."
Then he opened the door. The monk was going to challenge him. The Master immediately slapped his mouth.

64. The Way of Going Beyond

Jinfeng was once greeted by a monastic. Jinfeng grabbed the monastic and said, "The way of going beyond is not easy to attain." The monastic gestured to listen. Jinfeng then slapped him.
The monastic said, "Why did you slap me?"
Jinfeng said, "I want to have this kōan practiced."

65. The Unapproachable Zen Master

Master Mu-chou heard of an old Chan master who was practically unapproachable. He went to visit him. When the old Chan master saw Mu-chou entering his chamber, he immediately uttered, "Ho!" Mu-chou slapped him with his hand, and said, "What an imitation this is."
The old master said, "Where is my fault?"
Mu-chou scolded him, "You! You wild fox spirit!"
After saying this, Master Mu-chou returned home immediately.

66. The Meaning

The monk Fahui asked Master Mazu, 'What is the meaning of the Patriarch's coming from the West?'
'Shush! Keep your voice down,' said Mazu, 'come a little closer.'
Fahui came closer, whereupon Mazu gave him a slap in the face, saying, 'We are being overheard, come back tomorrow.'
Fahui came back the next day and entering the Dharma-hall, said, 'May the venerable monk please explain.'
Mazu said, 'Withdraw and wait for a little while until the old boy (Mazu referring to himself) has ascended
the rostrum. Then come forward and I will give you the confirmation of attainment.'
Fahui was suddenly awakened. He said, 'Thanks to the great assembly for the confirmation of attainment.' He walked once around the Dharma-hall and then left.

Fahui later on himself became a famous Zen Master.

67. Kill the Buddha

When Buddha was born, he took seven steps, looked in the four directions, pointed with one hand to the sky and with the other hand to the ground, and said, "I alone am the honored one above and below Heaven."

Somebody once mentioned these words of the baby Buddha to Zen Master Yunmen and asked what they meant. Yunmen said, "If I had seen what he did at that time, I would have killed him with a single blow and given him to a dog to eat up. And I would thus attempt to bring great peace to all under Heaven."

68. Hsueh-feng Rejects a Monk

A monk came to Hsueh-feng and made a formal bow. Hsueh-feng hit the monk five blows with the stick. At this the monk asked, "Where is my fault?"
With another five blows the master shouted at the monk to get out.

69. Three

Once when Master Yunmen was giving a talk he mentioned three kinds of people: "The first awakens when hearing a talk, the second awakens when called, and the third turns around and leaves when hearing that anything is brought up. Tell me, what does turning around and going away mean?"
Answering for the assembly, he said, "The third also deserves thirty blows."

70. Twenty Blows

One evening the Master Mu-chou Tao-tsung said to his assembly: "All of you! Those who do not yet have insight into Chan must seek it; those who do have it should not be ungrateful to me afterward." Just then a monk stepped out from the crowd, bowed,
and said, "I will never be ungrateful to you, sir!" The Master rebuked him, "You have already been ungrateful to me." The Master then said, "Ever since I came to preside here, I have not seen one man free from attachment. Why don't you come forward?" A monk then came up to him. The Master said, "My supervisor is not here, so you had better go outside the gate and give yourself twenty blows." The monk protested: "Where is my mistake?" The Master said, "You have added a lock to your cangue."

71. Guidance

A monk asked, "I just came to the assembly. Please give me guidance!"
The Master Mu-chou Tao-tsung: "You don't know how to ask a question."
The monk: "How would you ask it?"
The Master: "I will release you from thirty blows. Give them to yourself and get out of here."

72. Knowledge

'As to worldly knowledge and logical cleverness, I have nothing to do with them; pray let me have a Zen theme.' When this was asked by a monk, the master gave him a hearty blow.

73. Distinguish

A monk asked Hsing-hua: 'I am unable to distinguish black from white. Pray enlighten me somehow.' The question was hardly out when the master gave him a good slashing.

74. The Strange Book

The Meditator Chen Jianmin (1906-1987) has written a book called "The Lighthouse in the Ocean of Chan". This is the opening talk of that book:

"Who told you to open this book? What are you lacking of? You should be given thirty blows even before opening it. If you have taken it up on yourself already, and throw up upon encountering it, then you would be spared the shout that would deafen you for three months. Even though mentioning the koans, understand the sentence after Nirvana, the ultimate matter is still not there. Thirty blows, receive them yourself."

75. Beat Yourself with Stick

A Zen student came to Bankei and said: 'Master, I have an ungovernable temper -- how can I cure it?' 'Show me this temper,' said Bankei, 'It sounds fascinating.'

'I haven't got it right now,' said the student, 'so I can't show it to you.'

'Well then,' said Bankei, 'bring it to me when you have it.'

'But I can't bring it just when I happen to have it,' protested the student. 'It arises unexpectedly, and I would surely lose it before I got it to you.'

'In that case,' said Bankei, 'it cannot be part of your true nature. If it were, you could show it to me at any time. When you were born you did not have it, and your parents did not give it to you -- so it must come into you from the outside. I suggest that whenever it gets into you, you beat yourself with a stick until the temper can't stand it, and runs away.'

76. Punishing the Sky

A monk asked Zen Master Fen-yang, "If there is no bit of cloud in the sky for ten thousand miles, what do you say about it?"
"I would punish the sky with my stick," Fen-yang replied.
"Why do you blame the sky?" the monk persisted.
"Because," answered Fen-yang, "there is no rain when we should have it and there is no fair weather when we should have it."

77. I-chung Preaches Dharma

When master I-chung had taken his seat to preach Dharma, a layman stepped from the audience and walked from east to west in front of the rostrum. A monk then demonstrated his Zen by walking from west to east. "The layman understands Zen," said I-chung, "but the monk does not." The layman approached I-chung saying, "I thank you for your approval," but before the words were ended, he was struck with the master's stick. The monk approached and said, "I implore your instruction," and was also struck with the stick. I-chung then said, "Who is going to conclude this kōan?" No one answered. The question was repeated twice, but there was still no answer from the audience. "Then," said the master, "I will conclude it." He threw his stick to the floor and returned to his room.

78. Well-come or Ill-come?

Zen master Rinzai asked a nun, "Well-come or ill-come?" The nun shouted.
"Go on, go on, speak!" cried the master, taking up his stick.
Again, the nun shouted. The master hit her.

79. The Most Wonderful Thing

A monk came to Pai-chang and asked, "What is the most wonderful thing in the world?"
"I sit on top of this mountain," answered Pai-chang.
The monk paid homage to the teacher folding his hands palm to palm. At that moment Pai-chang hit the monk with his stick.

80. Shoushan's Stick

Shoushan Xingnian held up a bamboo stick and said to the assembly, "If you call it a stick, you defile it. If you don't call it a stick, you miss it. What do you call it?"
Shexian Guixing, who heard him, had great realization. He went close to Shoushan, snatched away the stick, and broke it in two. He threw the pieces down on the ground and said, "What is this?"
Shoushan said, "You blind fool!"
Shexian bowed.

81. The Stick

When the monk Yicun was practicing with Master Changqing Da'an on Mt. Gui, he once found an unusual twisted stick in the woods that was shaped like a snake. He presented it to the master, exclaiming how it had naturally taken such a striking shape, without any human carving. Da'an said, "Inhabitants of this mountain have no ax with which to carve it."

82. The Three Worlds Are Mind

Dizang was once asked by his teacher, Xuansha, "How do you understand that the three worlds are just one mind?"
Dizang pointed at a chair and said, "Master, what do you call this?"
Xuansha said, "A chair."
Dizang said, "You don't understand that the three worlds are just one mind."
Picking up a stick, Xuansha said, "I call this a bamboo stick. What do you call it?"
Dizang said, "I also call it a bamboo stick."
Xuansha said, "It's impossible to find a single person in the entire world who understands the Buddhadharma."

83. Staying in the Woods and Living on Herbs

Zen Master Tongda went into the Great White Mountains. He had no supply of grain, so when he was hungry, he ate herbs. He rested under the trees. He sat upright contemplating the mystery for five years without stopping. Once he happened to hit a clump of dirt with a stick, and when the clump of dirt broke up, he opened up in great enlightenment.

84. The Fist

Zen master Huitang Zuxin (1025-1100), when interviewing a monk in the abbot's quarters, would often raise a fist and say, "If you call it a fist, I'll hit you with it. If you don't call it a fist, you're being evasive. What do you call it?"

85. Guizong Holds Up a Fist

Once Guizong Zhichang was asked by Governor Libo, "I am not asking about the Three Vehicles and the Twelve Divisions of Sūtras. But what is the meaning of the Ancestor's [Bodhidharma's] coming from India?"
Guizong held up his fist and said, "Do you understand?"
Libo said, "No, I don't."
Guizong said, "You have studied extensively, yet you don't know what a fist is!"
Libo said, "Truly, I don't understand it."
Guizong said, "If you meet a true person, you are fulfilled in the Way. If you do not meet a true person, you spread worldly truth."

86. Weight

Once upon a time, a Korean Zen master, Kyong Ho, was traveling with his disciple, Man Gong, who had just become a Buddhist monk. The young disciple kept muttering about his heavy packs all the way and begged his master for a rest from time to time. But Zen Master Kyong Ho kept walking with a good spirit.

One day, while passing through a small village, they saw a woman leaving her house. Zen Master Kyong Ho, who was walking in front of his disciple, grabbed the woman's hand all of a sudden. The woman screamed and very soon her family and neighbors came to her help. They thought the master was sexually harassing the poor woman and started to chase after the two travelers, shouting and waving their fists. Zen Master Kyong Ho immediately turned around and fled desperately. The young disciple Man Gong ran like mad after his master, with packs on his back.

The two travelers kept running and running through trails and roads, until the villagers stopped chasing after them. The master suddenly stopped by a quiet pathway, turned around, and asked his disciple: "Still heavy now?"

"It's strange, Master. I don't even feel any heaviness of the packs while running."

87.   The Tao

A monk asked Pao-chi: "What is the Tao?"
"Come in," said the master.
"I don't understand," said the monk.
"Get out!" replied the master.

88. Fooling

Having entered the Dharma Hall for a formal instruction, Zen Master Yunmen said:
"Get out, get out of here! You're fooling each other without end!"
Then Master Yunmen asked the assembly: "Is even to say what I just said a mistake?"

89. What is One Plus Two??

One day long ago Seung Sahn Soen Sa asked all of his students, "One plus two equals what?"
One student replied, "One plus two equals three."
Soen Sa said, "No, one plus two is zero."
"Why zero? If you add two apples to one apple you will have three apples."
"If I eat one apple and two apples, then there are no apples."
"This isn't right."
"You say that one plus two equals three. I say one plus two equals zero. What is right?"
The student did not answer.
Soen Sa hit him and said, "A lion grabs and claws people; the dog only runs away with a
bone."
On another day, Soen Sa asked the students the same question: "What does one plus two
equal?"
One student shouted, "KATZ!"
"Is this the truth?"
"No, it is not the truth."
"What is the truth?"
"One plus two equals three."
"I understand that you are a blind dog, but now I see a keen-eyed lion."

90. You Idiots

Zen master Rinzai once said:
"Friends I tell you this: there is no Buddha, no spiritual path to follow, no training and no realization. What are you feverishly running after? Putting a head on top of your own head, you blind idiots! Your head is right where it should be. The trouble lies in your not believing in yourselves enough. Because you don't believe in yourselves you are knocked here and there by all the conditions in which you find yourselves. Being enslaved and turned around by objective situations, you have no freedom whatever, you are not masters of yourselves. Stop turning to the outside and don't be attached to my words either. Just cease clinging to the past and hankering after the future."

91. Fen-yang's Walking Stick

Zen Master Fen-yang brought forth his walking stick and said to his monks, "Whoever understands this walking stick thoroughly can end his traveling for Zen."

What Next?

Great that you finished these 91 Zen stories. What next?

The Zen Masters are the people who have spent a lot of time in meditation. Then only they preach others. If you just read the stories and do not meditate at all, you will miss the whole point. Go to different meditation centers. Try few meditation techniques and then find the one which suits you most. After a few months of practice, when you will read these same Zen stories, you will find many hidden meanings.

These stories are not something which you read once and forget. These stories carry the most pregnant wisdom available on earth. Work hard on meditation and revisit these stories again after some time. Perhaps then you will understand what I am pointing to!

Bibliography

1. Zen's Chinese Heritage by Andy Ferguson
2. Records of the Transmission of the Lamp (Jingde Chuandeng Lu, Vol. 1-6) by Daoyuan, translated by Randolph S. Whitfield
3. Treasury of the Forest of Ancestors by Satyavayu
4. 101 Zen Stories [Collection of Stone and Sand], Transcribed by Nyogen Senzaki & Paul Reps
5. Radical Zen (Recorded Sayings of Joshu) by Yoel Hoffman
6. Entangling Vines: A Classic Collection of ZEN Koans by Thomas Yuho Kirchner
7. The Blue Cliff Record
8. Shoyoroku
9. Records of Zen Master Rinzai
10. Dogen's 300 Koans
11. Zen Koans by Kubose
12. Zen Speaks: Shouts of Nothingness by Tsai Chih Chung
13. The Original Teachings of Ch'an Buddhism by Chang Ching Yuan
14. The Golden Age of Zen by John Ching Hsiung Wu
15. And the Flowers Showered by Osho
16. The Iron Flute: 100 Zen Koans by Nyogen Senzaki, Ruth Strout-McCandless
17. "Cultural Vs. Natural Behavior" discourse by Alan Watts
18. (Collected Works of Korean Buddhism, Volume 8) Seon Dialogues, Edited and Translated by John Jorgensen

www.ingramcontent.com/pod-product-compliance
Lightning Source LLC
Chambersburg PA
CBHW072059290426
44110CB00014B/1750